OVER HERE IT'S DIFFERENT

Carolina's Story

MILDRED LEINWEBER DAWSON
Photographs by GEORGE ANCONA

Macmillan Publishing Company
New York

Maxwell Macmillan Canada
Toronto

Maxwell Macmillan International
New York   Oxford   Singapore   Sydney

The author wishes to thank Dr. Roger Daniels, Professor of
History at the University of Cincinnati, for his assistance
in reviewing the manuscript.

Macmillan Publishing Company is part of the Maxwell
Communication Group of Companies.
Macmillan Publishing Company
866 Third Avenue
New York, NY 10022
Maxwell Macmillan Canada, Inc.
1200 Eglinton Avenue East
Suite 200
Don Mills, Ontario M3C 3N1
First edition
Printed in the United States of America
The text of this book is set in 13 pt. Century Book.
Book design by George Ancona
Prints by Gene Merinov of Aurora Color Labs, New York

10 9 8 7 6 5 4 3 2 1

Library of Congress Cataloging-in-Publication Data
Dawson, Mildred Leinweber. Over here it's different :
Carolina's story / Mildred Leinweber Dawson ;
photographs by George Ancona. — 1st ed.   p.   cm.
Summary: Relates, in text and photographs, the
experiences of an eleven-year-old girl who emigrated from
the Dominican Republic at age seven, and describes the
two worlds she lives in as an American trying to preserve
her heritage. ISBN 0-02-726328-2   1. Dominican
Americans—New York (N.Y.)—Juvenile literature. 2.
Dominicans (Dominican Republic)—New York (N.Y.)—
Juvenile literature. [1. Dominican Americans—New York
(N.Y.)] I. Ancona, George, ill. II. Title. E184.D6D38   1993
974.7'1004687293—dc20   92-44515

For my father, Philip S. Leinweber,
an immigrant child once,
and my mother, Pearl Leinweber,
and for Horace, Greeley, and Beverly
—M.L.D.

Para Tío Carlos y Tía Isolina
—G.A.

AUTHOR'S NOTE

"We are not a nation so much as a world," wrote novelist Herman Melville in the 1850s. He was describing the great variety of immigrants coming to America in his day, each one searching for a new life. Today, Melville's words still ring true.

Immigrants have come here from every country on earth. For each of them, the move has demanded courage, resilience, and flexibility. They must adapt to a new language, new foods, new customs, new neighbors. Many immigrants have become famous—to name a few, composer Irving Berlin (from Russia), basketball player Akeem Olajawon (from Nigeria), and physicist Albert Einstein (from Germany). The vast majority have been ordinary, hardworking Americans.

Our first wave of immigrants came in the 1700s, when our country was still a group of colonies. Settlers from England, Spain, and other nations encountered this continent's Native Americans. Africans were forcibly shipped here to work as slaves.

In the 1840s came the second wave—

Immigration and Naturalization Service official and public health official at immigration station, 1907

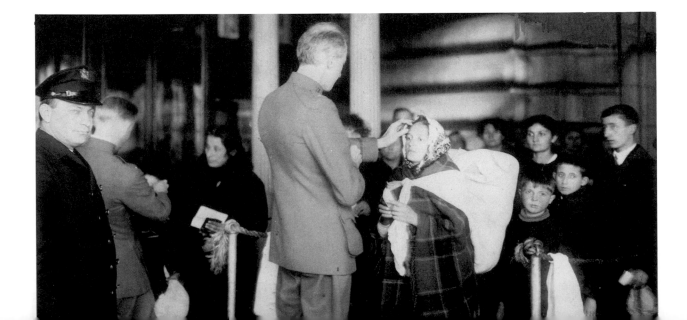

millions of Irish and German immigrants. They changed the religious makeup of our nation from an almost exclusively Protestant country to one with many Catholics and Jews. Chinese immigrants also started to arrive in large numbers in the 1840s and 1850s, joining the California Gold Rush.

During the third wave, between 1880 and 1914, twenty million Europeans came to the United States. Most were Catholic, Jewish, and Eastern Orthodox people who spoke no English; many of them were poor and illiterate.

Our country is now experiencing its fourth major wave of immigration. Nearly one million people move here yearly, mostly from Latin America and Asia. Unlike earlier immigrants, who came by boat, today's immigrants usually travel by airplane.

The Dominican Republic is among the top ten countries sending immigrants here. Between 1981 and 1990, nearly 252,000 people from the Dominican Republic moved north. One was a seven-year-old girl named Carolina Liranzo. This is her story.

Immigrant children, 1909

*C*arolina Liranzo, age eleven, lives in an apartment in Queens, a borough of the city of New York, with her father, stepmother, half brother, Delwin, and half sister, Daphne. Carolina goes to a school two blocks from her home, at PS (public school) 151.

Until she was seven, Carolina lived in the Dominican Republic, where her father grew up. The Dominican Republic is a small country. It occupies half of an island called Hispaniola, in the Caribbean Sea. (The other half of Hispaniola is Haiti.) The Dominican Republic is as big as Vermont and New Hampshire combined, but its population of seven million is several times larger than the combined population of those two states.

Carolina still remembers a great deal about the Dominican Republic. Although she misses aspects of life there and people she left behind—especially her grandfather—she feels very lucky to live in the United States. "I can learn so much more here," she says, "because my school offers classes in music and science and computers. They don't teach those things there. They can't afford to. The Dominican Republic is not like America, a very rich state. It is a very poor state."

Carolina always knew that one day she would be emigrating to the United States. (*Emigrating* means leaving your own country to go settle in another. *Immigrating*, in contrast, means coming into a new country with plans to stay.) Carolina knew because for years before she actually came to America, her father, Miguel Liranzo, was planning their move.

Carolina, 1983

Carolina and Miguel, 1980

Grandfather and Carolina, 1980

Carolina never really knew her biological mother. Her mother was a poor woman who had a relationship with Carolina's father; the two didn't marry. Carolina's grandparents—her father's parents—took her into their home in a small town called Laguna Salada when she was a baby, since they could better afford to care for her than her natural mother could. But Carolina always knew the woman her father eventually married, Maria. She knew her because Maria's grandparents live next door to Carolina's.

One reason Miguel wanted to go to America was that Maria already lived there. With her mother, Maria had moved from the Dominican Republic to the United States at the age of ten. Maria saw Miguel whenever she and her mother returned to the Dominican Republic for

Carolina and Grandmother, 1981

Miguel and Maria, 1983

visits. When they fell in love and decided to marry, Miguel and Maria agreed that they and their children could build a better life in America—that the family could be more prosperous in this country, and that the children could receive a better education.

At the time of their marriage, Maria was working and going to school in New York, and Miguel was still living in the Dominican Republic. For the wedding, Maria and all of the couple's Dominican friends in New York flew down to Laguna Salada. Carolina was only three at the time and remembers: "I was running around the church with a nice dress on." The wedding was held in a Catholic church since the Liranzos, like most Dominicans, are Catholic.

After the wedding, Maria returned to New York and began the slow process of obtaining permission for Miguel to join her. The United States government allows people to come to America for several reasons. One is to join close relatives who live here.

With the help of an immigration lawyer, Maria filed many forms. Also, she went to several interviews with officials who decide which foreigners can move here. Finally, she was successful. Almost a year and a half after their wedding, Miguel came to the United States. Only then could Maria ask the U.S. government for permission to bring Carolina here. Maria had to prove that Carolina was her stepdaughter, for whom she took full responsibility.

Again, gaining the government's approval took a long time. Carolina wasn't able to join Miguel and Maria in New York until more than three years after Miguel had immigrated.

The idea of moving to America excited Carolina. "She was really looking forward to coming here," Maria remembers. "The U.S. was something completely new, like another planet."

Carolina's flight to New York with Miguel, Maria, and Delwin (her half brother, who had been born two years before) was her first. "I wasn't scared," she says. "I thought flying would be like moving in the air, like being inside a bird's body."

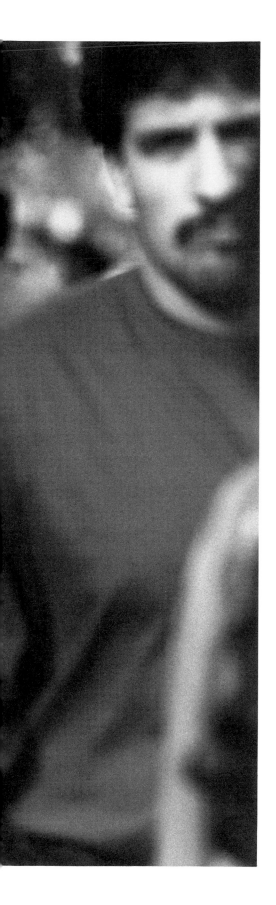

Carolina was startled by the dense crowds they encountered when they landed. The size and population of New York, compared to her small, uncrowded old home, was a difference—the first of many—to which she had to adapt. Even though it is not so, it seemed to Carolina that "in the little island of Manhattan alone, there are more people than there are in the whole Dominican Republic."

One month after Carolina arrived here, she says, "I just wanted to go back." She sorely missed her grandfather. "When I left the Dominican Republic, I cried because I hated to leave him," she says.

Carolina was glad, though, to finally join Miguel, Maria, and Delwin. In Queens, Carolina's family lived in a small apartment in a six-story building without any outdoor play space for children. In Laguna Salada, Carolina had lived in a big, airy house with a good-sized, shady yard. Right next to the house was a café run by her grandparents, where she also spent a lot of time. The yard had lemon trees and tamarind trees (her grandmother made the tamarind fruit into juice and ice cream). Carolina and a group of her cousins, some of whom lived with her grandparents, as she did, others of whom lived close by, played together under the trees most of every day.

The cousins who lived with Carolina, all boys, were the sons of her father's sisters. Her Aunt Lourdes, Tía Lourdes in Spanish, had gotten divorced and returned to live in the home of her parents. With her had come her four sons: Rae, Gabriel, Toni, and Ramon. Tía Chiqui (pronounced *Chee-key*) and her one child, a son named Christian, were living with her parents until she could move to New York.

Carolina and her cousins invented games. They liked to tie old sheets to tree branches, making hammocks to swing in. They played make-believe games, too, pretending to be parents or teachers.

When Carolina first arrived in Queens, she had no cousins nearby with whom she could play. Since she was one of the first Liranzo children to emigrate, she felt that Queens was "a lonely place—there weren't any kids around." Two-year-old Delwin didn't really count; he was too little. "Also, I had more freedom over there, at my grandpa's house," Carolina says. "In New York, I can't play outside much except in summer because it's cold most of the year and school takes so much time. In the Dominican Republic, it's always warm and I didn't spend so much time in school."

Carolina soon discovered that New York kids often stay indoors for another reason: television. "Children here watch a lot of cartoons," Carolina says. They also watch tapes on their VCRs. Carolina's grandparents did not own a VCR. "It cost too much," she explains, "and we didn't know where we could buy tapes. Also, electricity was always a problem there."

Unlike Queens, where a power outage happens very rarely, in Laguna Salada there were frequent brownouts and blackouts, times when the power would drop or go off. "I hated the blackouts because it got so dark we would bump into things," Carolina recalls. (The water went off so often that her grandparents always kept jars and pails filled with water.)

Carolina had to get used to new foods here. Although Maria often cooks many of the same spicy dishes that Carolina ate in Laguna Salada, Dominican food is not served at most restaurants or in school, where Carolina buys lunch every day. "Carolina just wouldn't touch hot dogs, hamburgers, or pizza when she first got here," Maria says. "But eventually she saw that the other kids liked those foods, and we tried to make her taste them. Gradually she started accepting them."

Even very simple foods, such as orange juice and milk, tasted strange to Carolina in New York. "I didn't like the milk here. It was hard for me to drink it," Carolina says. "Over there, we just took the milk straight from the cow—it tasted a little salty—and I would usually drink it warm. It's not like the milk here, that we always drink cold." As for orange juice, she explains, "We drank orange juice for breakfast, but not the kind they sell here—it was orange juice you made from oranges."

Rice and beans form the mainstay of the Liranzo family's diet in New York, as they did in the Dominican Republic. The family also eats other starchy vegetables that are popular throughout the Caribbean: plantains and yuccas. Plantains look like large green bananas, but are always eaten cooked. Yuccas, (sometimes called *cassavas*), resemble potatoes but are, Maria says, "harder and tastier." On the weekends, when Maria is not working and has more time, she prepares *sancocho*, a rich stew of chicken, beef, and pork, with carrots and other vegetables. Carolina enjoys these Dominican dishes, although American-born Delwin does not.

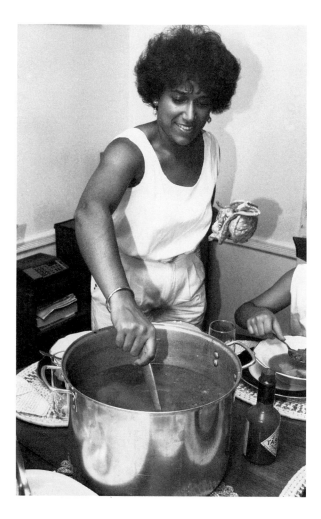

Another big adjustment for Carolina was the change in languages. In the Dominican Republic, she spoke only Spanish, the language of that country. At PS 151, all the teachers and students speak English. Having to learn English was a tremendous pressure for Carolina, as it is for most immigrants. "I remember that once, when I first got here, I took a book and started saying things that didn't mean anything. I was making believe I was speaking English. In school, I felt like I was the only one from another country. It wasn't really true, but I was the newest."

Actually, many students at PS 151 come from other countries. In Carolina's class alone, there are children from Romania, Portugal, and China.

Luckily, there were many kind children at school who spoke both Spanish and English, and they translated for Carolina. "A lot of people helped me by explaining to the teacher what I meant when I spoke in Spanish," she remembers. "And when the teacher answered me in English, my friends would tell me in Spanish what she had said." Watching American television also added to her English vocabulary.

Miguel and Maria could have sent Carolina and Delwin to a school where Spanish is the main language of instruction. In that school, children whose first language is Spanish study English as a second language. "But we don't agree with that approach," Maria says. "The children never really pick up English that way."

Although Carolina's parents send their children to the English-speaking school, they do want them to be fluent in Spanish. Miguel is adamant about his children maintaining a firm hold on the language and values of the Dominican Republic.

"Miguel loves his Dominican flag so much. He wants the children to keep our culture and traditions," says Maria. "He sometimes forbids Delwin to speak English at home, or at least around him."

Six-year-old Delwin slips into English constantly, and this angers his father. Maria adds that both she and Miguel have been surprised—and slightly alarmed—to observe that sometimes "even Carolina won't know simple Spanish words that she used to know."

Carolina confirms this. "Sometimes I have to ask, How do you say *scissors*? How do you say *ear*?"

A Hispanic value that Carolina's parents stress is respect for elders. (Hispanic is a descriptive word that means of Spain or Latin America.) "Both Miguel and I come from very strict families," Maria says, "where children learn that if adults are having a conversation, they are not supposed to butt in." Carolina and Delwin follow that rule.

There is, though, one aspect of Hispanic culture that the Liranzos are not stressing. It is "macho" thinking. "Macho" is short for the Spanish word *machismo*. People with macho attitudes believe that men and boys are entitled to special privileges, respect, and power.

When Maria was growing up, macho thinking prevailed in her own family. Because of it, her brothers never did housework. They played all day, while the girls and women did all the chores. Maria and Miguel don't believe that this is right. Miguel helps with cooking and cleaning when he can, and Maria tries to assign chores at home to both Carolina and Delwin. Carolina ends up doing a lot more housework only because Delwin, at age six, is not as responsible. Instead of cleaning his room when he is supposed to, Delwin usually plays with his cousin Jose.

Jose is one of several of Carolina's cousins who live in her building. Jose happens to have been born here, but most of the cousins, like Carolina, emigrated with their parents.

Just as Miguel and Maria did, Carolina's aunts, uncles, and cousins have all received a great deal of help from her grandparents in moving north. The grandparents take care of the children left behind, making it possible for the aunts and uncles to go ahead and get settled in New York. Then, when the parents are comfortably situated, with a home and a job, they go back to get their children. (Only Carolina's grandmother, whom she adores, visits the family in New York. Her grandfather refuses to come, preferring to see his children and grandchildren when they visit him.)

And so, participating in "chain migration" (in which members of a family, clan, or village immigrate one after another, like links in a chain), the entire younger generation of Liranzos is gradually moving to America. As Maria says, "One by one, they come."

In their steady shift northward to America, the Liranzo family is typical of people from the Dominican Republic. The Dominican Republic now sends more immigrants to the United States than does any other Caribbean nation.

Carolina and the other children think that it is great to live so close to one another. It means they have many different apartments in the building where they can play. Two-year-old Daphne especially loves running from one apartment to the next.

Carolina, Delwin, Daphne, Miguel, and Maria live in an apartment on the first floor. One of Carolina's newly arrived aunts, Tía Chiqui, is staying with them while she looks for work. Her son, Christian, is there, too. The Liranzos have had a steady stream of family members living with them while the new immigrants find their own apartment.

Tía Lourdes and her four sons have moved into an apartment on the second floor. Still another aunt, Tía Graciela, lives there, with her fifteen-year-old daughter, Massiel, who is Carolina's favorite cousin. Maria's brother, Jose Peña, and his wife, Eugenia, also live in a second-floor apartment.

The Liranzos and their relatives help one another a lot. This closeness and willingness to share that exists between members of her extended family is something that has remained constant for Carolina in both places she has lived.

Miguel and Maria help the newly arrived relatives to learn English, settle into new apartments and schools, and find jobs. The relatives give the Liranzos a great deal of support, too. For instance, even though both Miguel and Maria work full-time, they never pay for child care, as most working parents do. An aunt or older cousin is always available to watch Carolina, Delwin, and Daphne as a favor.

The Liranzos and their relatives also have a lot of fun together. On weekends, they all get together in one of the apartments to cook big family meals. And usually they go out together. Sometimes they go sight-seeing in New York, to destinations like the top of the Empire State Building or the World Trade Center. Often they go to visit Miguel's sister, Mercedes. She lives with her husband, Cesar, and their children in Washington Heights, a Manhattan neighborhood that is home to a great many Dominican people. Maria says, "The aunts love to go uptown because there everybody speaks their language."

The Liranzos also enjoy spending holidays and most family birthdays together, either in Queens or in Manhattan. For Mother's Day, they often go in a big group to see Maria's mother, who lives in Brooklyn. The family now celebrates Christmas in the traditional American way, with presents under a brightly trimmed tree. They always leave their tree up, though, until January 6, which in Hispanic countries is an important holiday called the Celebration of the Three Kings.

In Laguna Salada, January 6 was the day that Carolina received her gifts. The way she remembers it, "Santa wasn't the one who left toys. It was people from the desert who came under the door and left the presents at the bottom of the bed. The children would get ready for them by putting grass for them to rest on around the floor at the foot of the bed, and also a glass of water. The desert people would drink the water and leave the presents for you to find when you woke up." Maria explains that this is Carolina's interpretation of the Dominican custom. Most people say that the hay and water are food and drink for the camels ridden by the three kings when they went into the desert seeking the baby Jesus.

Another difference between Christmas in the two countries, Carolina says, is that "over there, we didn't get so many presents as we do here—one or two. Kids over there don't get a lot of gifts. If they ever went to Toys 'R' Us, they'd just die!"

Birthdays had a different, quieter feeling in the Dominican Republic, too. There, Carolina remembers, "We would celebrate my birthday at night. My grandma would buy a cake and put a doll on top of it. My cousins and friends would come over and we would play cards and tag."

Maria makes a much bigger production out of the children's parties. Daphne's last party, for instance, was held at McDonald's. Maria hired a party coordinator who organized special games, and she put up a piñata. A piñata is a hollow papier-mâché creature that is filled with toys and candies. It is hung from the ceiling by a rope so that children can break it apart with a stick, releasing all the goodies inside.

Now that Carolina is older, her birthday celebrations include music and dancing. "I like rap music, Spanish music, all kinds of music," she says. In New York, though, just as in Laguna Salada, Carolina always has a Dominican birthday cake. Maria orders it from a bakery in Washington Heights. Many of the foods sold there are unavailable elsewhere in New York. Compared to American birthday cakes, "ours are bigger, much more moist, and more elaborately decorated," says Maria.

Not only on birthdays, but whenever members of Carolina's family crave special foods from their home, they can go buy them in Washington Heights. There they find *salchichón*, a spicy sausage somewhat like a less oily pepperoni, and *chicharrón*, fried pork with the skin left on, which is served with lots of salt. Carolina likes *mondongo*, a soup made with the stomach of a cow or pig, although American-born Delwin will not touch it.

Carolina has learned much more about cooking and about all other kinds of housework since she came to Queens. Her parents need her help around the house far more than her grandparents did. Carolina's grandparents, like most other middle-class people in the Dominican Republic, had several servants to help them with household chores. Carolina remembers one: "This girl named Mayra cleaned the house. If I felt like helping, I helped—but I didn't have to."

Maria explains that in the Dominican Republic, "If you are comfortably well off, you take a little girl from a poor family and you bring her up and she helps you in the house. That's how Mayra came to Carolina's grandparents. They had other people come in to wash and iron the clothes, too. So Carolina wasn't doing much housework down there.

"Here, though, she helps me a lot," Maria says. "She is learning to cook. She knows how to fry the plantains and prepare the rice. She cleans, too, mops the floors and makes the beds."

In Laguna Salada, Carolina helped her grandparents in a different way. Their small café next to the house is well located, since their property is on a corner near a busy street. Lots of people driving or walking by stop in for a snack or a cool drink. "I would take orders," Carolina says. "When people came in, I would ask them what they'd like. Then I would go tell my grandfather and he would put it on a tray for me to take to them."

The café was a congenial place, open most of the day. Neighbors and friends often dropped in. With her grandparents' permission, Carolina would snack on the cookies, cheeses, candies, and drinks they sold.

In a big back room of the restaurant, Carolina's grandfather shows movies. "My uncle goes to Santiago, a city that's an hour away, and rents them for my grandfather," Carolina says. "Over there, people don't go to movies in movie theaters."

In Queens, Carolina does not lead the same kind of leisurely life. Weekdays here are very busy for Carolina and her family. Miguel leaves the house every weekday morning by seven o'clock to go to his job in Manhattan. He works as an auto mechanic for a car dealer. He also rents garage space near their home in Queens, to which he goes when he leaves his day job. There, in the evenings and on weekends, he repairs cars for neighbors. Miguel is building up his own auto repair business and hopes someday to work only for himself.

Maria wakes up at 7:00 A.M. Before going to work, she cooks food that Carolina will reheat for dinner. The night before, Maria gets all the ingredients ready so that she can prepare the dishes easily in the morning.

Carolina and Delwin rise at 7:15 A.M. Carolina sleeps in a bedroom she shares with Daphne, and there is often a recently arrived cousin or aunt there, too. (In the Dominican Republic, she slept in a little bed in the corner of her grandparents' room, and her grandfather's loud snoring often startled her awake.) Delwin has his own room, next to Carolina's.

At around 8:15, Carolina, Delwin, and Jose, Maria's nephew, leave for school with Maria. After dropping the children off, Maria, who is a legal secretary, rides the subway to her job in Manhattan.

After school, Gladys Fuentes, a friend of the family's who lives in their building, picks up the children. She stays with them until Maria comes home. The children do homework and, for Carolina, there are also many chores. She helps watch Delwin and Daphne, and when it is almost time for Maria to return home, she sets the table for dinner. She then reheats the food Maria cooked in the morning so that the children and Maria can eat when Maria comes home at 6:00 P.M. Miguel does not usually return home until about eight o'clock.

In Laguna Salada, Carolina had more free time because her grandparents did not send her to school regularly. Maria says, "They spoiled her—treated her like a princess and allowed her to stay home. We thought she was going to school, but we now know that she was not going much. Over there, people don't value education the way we do here—they don't see it as so important. And the authorities there are not so strict."

Although Carolina appreciates and enjoys school now, when she started at PS 151, she found going

to a strange new school—for a long school day—very stressful. "I was scared when I first got there," Carolina explains. "I thought I would never learn to read and I would never have friends."

At first, Carolina's parents had to push her to get ready each school day. "She wouldn't dress or brush her teeth. It was a very difficult time for her and us," Maria remembers. "But she has made incredible progress—her teachers speak about it—and now she is a very hard worker. She has also made a lot of friends at school."

Carolina attends school from 8:40 A.M. until 3:00 P.M. In Laguna Salada, the school day was far shorter: "My classes started at eight o'clock in the morning and ended at noon. Then other kids went from one o'clock until five o'clock," she remembers.

In Laguna Salada, teachers did not give homework either. Carolina says, "There, when you read about science or social studies, you didn't study it deeply because you didn't have to do homework in the subject." In Queens, her teachers give her homework daily, except Fridays.

Carolina prefers the New York school system. She is happy to spend long hours at school here because the time is filled with subjects and activities that she enjoys and never experienced in Laguna Salada. "Over there," she says, "they teach you to read and write words, but they don't teach a lot of math, science, or social studies. And the kids don't usually get computers. They cost too much and the electricity is always a problem—going off all the time." Currently, Carolina's favorite subjects are writing and science.

The classrooms at PS 151 are more inviting than those at her school in Laguna Salada. "There were no bulletin boards in my classroom over there, with special displays to look at. The walls were just painted, or they might have had maps on them." Her classrooms now are lively—the walls have informative posters, and interesting study materials are out on display. In her science classroom, for instance, there are printed posters about different branches of science and posters the children made themselves. There is a globe, a model of the planets, microscopes, and live animals to observe.

The children at PS 151 also have ample supplies for art and science projects, and blank books in which they write and illustrate their own stories. Such materials were unavailable in Laguna Salada. "There was no big paper for drawing—only loose-leaf paper—and no crayons. They didn't have a library or bookshelves full of books like we have here. My old school didn't have an auditorium, a lunchroom, or a gym."

For Carolina, one great aspect of the long school day in New York is more time with friends. Evangelina, whose family comes from Greece, is a special friend because she and Carolina grew close soon after Carolina started at PS 151. But Carolina considers Tinisha, whose family comes from Jamaica, her "best, best buddy." Carolina and Tinisha walk in the halls together and sit beside each other at lunch. Sometimes they talk on the phone—to catch up on what happened in school if one of them was absent, or just to chat. Tinisha is the only friend Carolina phones.

Carolina's main teacher is Mrs. McKenna, but she studies special subjects in different classrooms with different teachers. For writing she has Miss Fox; for science, Miss Silverman, and for other subjects, such as family living and computers, still other teachers. Carolina likes the variety. "In my old school," she remembers, "we sat with one teacher in one classroom and we didn't study so many subjects."

Carolina finds her teachers in Queens kinder
than her teachers were in the Dominican
Republic. "Here teachers don't scream at you.
They treat you like they're your parents, they
help you," Carolina says. "They never put a
hand on you here—they were meaner at my
other school."

Carolina lists her New York school as one reason she is glad to live in America. She also likes the clothes here better. "They didn't have so many designs there," she says. Getting to play in snow sometimes is yet another benefit of living in New York.

Still, Carolina is not sure whether or not she wants to become an American citizen. "It may depend on who I marry," she says. She has years and years to decide.